CASH READY ALWAYS

Squeezing More Cash From Your Financial Statements

Table of Contents

Legal Notice

Disclaimer NoticeIntroduction

Chapter One: What is Cash Flow? How Cash Flows in a Business?

Chapter Two: What is the Current Situation of Cash? What Ratio Analysis is Needed?

Chapter Three: What is the Business Breakeven Point in Cash? What are the Steps to Calculate Breakeven?

Chapter Four: P&L - What can Change to Improve Cash?

Chapter Five: B/S - What can Change to Improve Cash?

Chapter Six: Cash Flow Statement - What can Change to Improve Cash?

Chapter Seven: Summary

Conclusion

Introduction

I want to thank you for choosing this book, *'Cash Ready Always - Squeezing More Cash From Your Financial Statements'* and hope you find the book informative.

When it comes to operating a business, it is important to manage the cash that flows in. Cash is the backbone of every business and, without it, the business will not work. However, it is easier said than done, as it is quite difficult to maintain a consistent cash flow. One way of managing it is by modifying financial documents.

Documents such as profit and loss statement, cash flow statement, balance sheet, etc. can be used to increase the cash that flows into the company.

In this book, we will look at some of how to modify these financial statements to remain with cash all year round.

Let us begin!

Chapter One: What is Cash Flow? How Cash Flows in a Business?

Cash flow refers to the net value of cash or cash-equivalents that move in and out. Cash flow is one of the main aspects that govern how well a business does. If it indicates a positive cash flow, then it means the company's liquid assets are on the rise and the company can settle the debts. It also has enough free cash to reinvest into the business and can return the sum to investors and shareholders. It will also have the chance to repay expenses and be prepared to take on all future expenses.

If there happens to be a negative cash flow, then it means the company's cash assets are going down in value. The net cash flow is different from the net income. It includes accounts receivable and other things for which payment is pending. The cash flow statement is required to know how much income the company is earning and how liquid its assets are. This will tell people how solvent or insolvent the company is.

The cash accrual system helps companies to assess their financial position in advance. This is done by counting credit as a part of the company's income. The accounts receivable and money due will appear in the assets part of the company's balance sheet. However, these items will only represent incomplete transactions that have taken place and will not be counted as cash. Note that any proceeds from cash transactions will be considered as cash just after they have been transferred.

On the other hand, a company can receive lots of cash inflow by disposing of its long-term assets. The company does so to increase its liquidity and limit its growth in the long term. However, this is the wrong approach to take as it can lead to business failure. In a sense, the company can take in cash by issuing bonds and balance out some of the instability and control the rise in debts. So, to solve this issue, it helps to go through the cash flow statement and balance sheet of a company along with the income statement.

Cash flow statement

The cash flow statement is better known as the statement of cash flows. This statement is used to check whether a company's income is sustainable and translating to cash flow or to struggle to remain consistent. All companies turn insolvent if they fail to have enough cash and cash equivalent available to settle their liabilities-both long term and short term.

If the company ties its profits to accounts receivables, paid expenses and the existing inventory, then it will not have the liquidity required to remain up during a downward phase of the business or when a lawsuit has been issued.

The cash flow of the business determines the amount of money that will flow into the business and the quality of it. If the net cash flow tends to be lower than the net income, then it can lead to issues.

The cash flow statement is split into three main sections namely operating cash flow, investing cash flow and financing cash flow. The operating cash flow relates to a company's day to day functioning. The investing cash flow is the investment made into the business through the acquisition of long-term assets. The financing cash flows relate to a company's investor and creditors. All the dividends paid out to stockholders is recorded here and the cash proceeds that are acquired after issuing the bonds.

If you wish to thoroughly understand the basics of cash flow to modify it to your advantage, then you have to know some terminologies that will help you along the way.

Free cash flow refers to a company's operating cash flow minus expenditures. It is this money that is used to pay off dividends, buy back stocks and pump money towards business expansion. It is a category that appears in the cash flow statement of a company that mentions external activities used to raise capital for a firm and pay back the investors by issuing cash dividends and through the issuance of more stock. The cash flow acquired through financial activities is used to showcase the strength of investors and the financial stability.

Those companies that regularly turn towards debt equity to have consistent cash flow tend to have issues in case the capital markets turn less liquid. The formula used to calculate cash flow from financial activities is as follows.

Cash received through the issuance of stock or debt minus cash paid as dividends and the re-acquisition of the debt or stock.

Cash flow from financial activities

If a large amount of cash flows into a business through financial activities, then it indicates that the company is doing well and the money flowing in and out of the company is balanced.

Any negative number will indicate that the company is having debt and can also mean that the company is making dividend payments or stock repurchases that will interest the investors. Investors will also have the chance to get first-hand information about the cash that is flowing in from financial activities by assessing the balance sheet equity and long-term debt. Cash flowing from financial activities happens to be one of the three main sections of a company's cash flow statement along with cash flow from operations and cash flow from investments. This part of the cash flow statement is used to measure the cash moving from the firm to the owners and creditors.

Business activities that help in creating positive cash flow include the likes of cash from issuing stock and receiving cash through the issuance of bonds. There can also be some business activities that generate a negative cash flow such as spending the cash to buy back previously issued stock or to pay debts and interest accrued on debts and paying off dividends etc.

Some companies have a cash flow coming in from business activities mentioned in their 10-K report that is given out to shareholders. A company will mention it as a repurchase of 2 million shares at an average of $5 per share and paid out $2 million to shareholders as dividends and used $1 million to pay debts and received $2 million from issuing lower-interest bonds.

Chapter Two: What is the Current Situation of Cash? What Ratio Analysis is Needed?

As discussed in the previous chapter, the cash flow statement happens to be a significant financial statement that is used by business operators in analyzing the cash flow. The cash flow is separate from the profit, and net income and the business operators must consider each and analyze them in diverse ways. There is some financial analysis that can help businesses focus on the final profit and the cash that flows in. The cash flow analysis happens to be one such ratio that calculates the flow of cash and how liquid the assets of the company are. To help you understand the importance of the cash flow statements, here are some of them.

Operating cash flow ratio

Operating cash flow refers to an analysis of how the money tends to move in and out of a company and how the business repays the debts and bills. The operating cash flow is a measure of the cash that flows into a company through its business operations and the liquidity of the assets in the short run. It is directly related to the debts owed by the company and the cash that flows in from the various businesses activities that are carried out.

Operating cash flow ratio = cash flows from operation and current liabilities.

A Cash flow from operations is taken from the cash flow statement, and current liabilities are taken from the balance sheet.

If the operating cash flow ratio happens to be less than 1.0 then the company might not be making enough cash to repay short-term debts and can lead to a serious issue. The company might also have to stop operations.

Price flow ratio

Price to cash flow ratio is used to measure a company's value of price to earnings per ratio. It is usually used as a ratio to know how a company is doing. It takes into account the company's share price to cash flow on a per share basis.

Here is a formula to calculate the price ratio

Price/cash flow ratio = share price/operating cash flow per share

Here, the share price is the closing price of the stock on a specific day and operating cash flow is summarized from the cash flow statement. Some businesses make use of free cash flow in the denominator in place of operating cash flow.

Most analysts still make use of price per earnings ratio while evaluating.

Cash flow margin ratio

Cash flow margin ratio is quite a remarkable ratio. It correlates the relationship that exists between the cash that is made from sales and business activities. A company requires cash to pay off dividends and settle debts with suppliers and make investments in new places. This means that cash happens to be on the same level as profits for a firm.

The cash flow margin ratio is used to measure the ways in which a business can convert its sales into cash income. The following formula is used

Cash flow from operating cash flow=___%

The numerator used in the equation is taken from the cash flow statement. The denominator is taken from the income statement. The greater the percentage value, the better it is.

Cash flow from operations

Cash flow from operations and average total liabilities is a ratio that is similar to the total debt to total asset ratio. Both are used to measure the liquidity capacity of a company to pay off its debts and keep itself afloat. The cash flow margin ratio is a better tool to use as it helps in measuring the ability of a business in staying afloat over a longer period.

The ratio to calculate is as follows

Cash flows from operations or average total liabilities=___%

Here, cash flow from operations is taken from the statement of cash flow and average total liabilities is the average of total liabilities taken from over different time periods and taken from the balance sheet.

The higher the ratio, the better is it for the firm and the flexible it remains in paying off debts.

Current ratios

The current ratio is one of the simplest cash flow ratios. It is used by business analysts to check whether the current assets are good enough to pay off the current debts. The ratio used is as follows

Current ratio = current assets/current liabilities=___X

Here, all the required information is taken from the balance sheet. The resulting answer showcases the number of times that a company meets its short-term debt and is also a measure of the firm's liquidity.

Quick ratio

The quick ratio is a specific test used to measure the liquidity of the current ratio. It removes inventory from the equation and measures a business's liquidity in case it does not have any inventory to sell and make for short-term obligations. If the quick ratio happens to be lesser than 1.0 times then it has to dispose of inventory to settle the short-term debts. But this is not a good position to be in for any company.

Quick ratio = current assets-inventory/current liability when all terms are taken away from the balance sheet.

Chapter Three: What is the Business Breakeven Point in Cash? What are the Steps to Calculate Breakeven?

Break-even point is used to know the volume of sales that are required to cover the operating expenses. If the sales are equal to the break-even point then the business will neither receive a profit nor will it suffer a loss. If the company is unable to attain a breakeven point then the company will suffer a loss. If the company happens to suffer from a loss then it does not always mean that the company will struggle to pay off its monthly and weekly debts such as bills and wages. The problem can be solved by calculating the breakeven point, and the formula for it is as follows.

Breakeven point in units=fixed costs/selling price per unit-variable cost per unit.

Here, fixed costs include all non-cash expenses including depreciation and amortization of the expenses that do not require cash payments in the short-term. The company, therefore, leaves it out. If the cash costs are made a part of the fixed costs then we arrive at the cash breakeven point.

Cash breakeven point=fixed costs-non-cash expenses/selling price per unit-variable cost per unit.

Cash break-even analysis

A cash break-even analysis is a comparison that is almost same to a typical break-even analysis. The only difference between the two is the cash break-even study takes out non-cash expenses thereby bringing about a varying result and providing analysts with an additional statistic and closer look at a firm's financial stand.

Cash break-even

The cash break-even point showcases a firm's minimum level of revenue from sales that is required to make the business attain a positive cash flow. A cash break-even study begins at the cash break-even point. To calculate it, you have to start by subtracting a company's fixed costs from depreciation. The result is divided by the margin of contribution per unit. The contribution margin is equivalent to the sales price of a single unit of the product minus the variable costs required to make a unit.

Companies usually suffer from a cash crunch. This is because holding on to cash equates to letting go of opportunities that can give the company a chance to grow. With the use of cash break-even analysis, a group can find the level of sales it requires to create to cover all cash expenses during a certain period.

Fixed costs and depreciation

To estimate the break-even point of cash, devaluation charges should be taken out, as they do not include cash payments. While calculating the cash break-even point, if it happens to be lower than the standard breakeven point then the depreciation is subtracted, and the fixed base is lowered.

Here is an example for the same.

Assume that a company sells its products for $20 each and has a variable cost of $10 to produce each unit. In addition to it, the company also has a fixed cost of $30,000 and $1000 of it is depreciation. The calculation takes place by setting per unit cost at $20 per unit cost equal to the sum of the $10 per unit variable cost and fixed costs minus depreciation that is $29,000. The equation is again done by deducting the $10 variable cost per unit from each of the equation to set the $10 per unit cost that is equivalent to the $29,000 net fixed costs. By dividing each side of the equation by the $10 unit cost this comes up to 2900. This tells us that the company has to sell at least 2900 units of the product at $20 to break even.

The breakeven analysis is done to find the exact point where the revenue that is received is equal to the cost that is accrued while receiving the revenue. Break-even analysis is used to calculate a margin of safety, which happens to be the amount of the revenue, exceeds the breakeven point. In other words, it is the amount of revenue that will fall and still remain above the breakeven point. Break-even analysis is a supply analysis and analyses the cost of sales. It does not take into account that the demand can be affected at varying price levels.

Say for example it takes $30 to make a widget and the fixed cost is $2,000. A fixed cost refers to the cost that does not vary with an increase or a decrease in the level of goods and services that are produced. The fixed costs happen to be expenses that a company has to pay regardless of the business it carries out. The costs are one of the most critical elements of the goods and services. Take for example a fixed cost would be a company's monthly rent for the building. If the company accrues a bill of $5,000 as rent and fails to make anything then the payment will be due in full.

As per the economic analysis, a business will achieve economies of scale when it manages to produce enough goods to cover fixed costs. Say for example $200,000 lease spread over 200,000 products then each product will have $1 as the fixed cost. If the company can make 400,000 products, the fixed cost will drop to 50 cents.

The variable costs depend on the rate of production. They will go up and fall as the production goes up and down. The variable costs are different from fixed costs and tend to remain constant no matter the output.

Variable costs usually includes material costs and labor costs that are required to finish a project. Say, for example, a business has variable costs that are associated with the promotion of its products. As and when the company promotes this product the costs will keep adding. On the other hand, if the company discontinues the product then its promotion costs comes to zero.

A concept known as semi-variable cost refers to a mix of the fixed costs and its variable components. These costs are fixed to a certain level and then turn variable once the level exceeds. In the case of semi-variable costs, the greater levels of production tend to go up in cost but if there is no production then the cost will still come through.

Labor costs are considered to be semi-variable costs by a business. The salaries and wages that are paid out to laborers might be fixed for some and variable for others. In some cases, the variable portion will be the extra that will be paid to employees in case they put in extra hours.

Remember that all businesses have to calculate their breakeven point if they wish to make the most of their business opportunities. As a reminder, the breakeven point is the point at which the total earnings equals the total costs or expenditure. There will be no profit or loss and the business breaks even.

Here are some reasons that make calculating breakeven points important

- It can help you know how important your business is and how your product line will fare
- Sometimes, a business might turn over quite a lot of money, but that does not mean it is making profits. It is therefore important to know the breakeven point to determine the margin of profit
- The breakeven point is used to check how far the sales will go down before the company begins to incur a loss
- It helps in determining how many units of the product has to be sold for the company to start making profits
- It showcases how reducing the number of sales can impact profits
- How much increase in the price or the volume of sales can help one increase the fixed costs

There can be many ways in which you can calculate the breakeven point. We looked at the different ways, and you can use any of them to calculate your business break even.

Chapter Four: P&L - What can Change to Improve Cash?

Profit and loss statement is a financial statement that makes a note of your business income and profits, costs incurred, expenses, etc. This can be prepared for each quarter or the whole year.

The profit and loss statement is used to seek information that showcases how much money has come into the company and how many expenses have been accrued. The statement is mostly used to know how a company can reduce the costs and increase the profits.

In case you wish to apply for a loan for your company's development then you will have to submit your profit and loss statement within three months of submitting your application. So, it is mandatory to update your statement every month so that you know exactly where the company stands.

Most banks will also ask for your profit and loss statement to keep track of your business and maintain records. It will help them assess the historical and current profitability and maintain a record of the way in which cash flows into your business and your ability in paying off debts. To achieve this, you have to review your cash flow statement regularly and review your profit and loss statements. You might at this point think that the profit and loss statement and cash flow are related, but they are not.

Profit and loss statement is based on the accrual as compared to the cash flow statement, which is based on cash receivable. The two are interrelated to a great extent but not the same. A profit and loss statement will give you a clear idea of how certain activities will work out and the level of income and expenditure that will be incurred over a certain period. If a company fails to prepare a profit and loss statement then they will not know where they are headed.

Ideally, the profit and loss statement should be prepared for one to three years in advance. For this, you have to create a profit and loss statement on a monthly basis for the first year and then quarterly for the next two years.

You can make use of the newest technologies that make it easy to maintain records and books. Software can be downloaded on to your computer, and you can start maintaining the records. In fact, good software can help you manage managerial efficiency and might also promote efficient work balance and help your business grow. There are some that will help you adopt ways in which to increase cash flow.

If you begin to notice that your sales are increasing but profits are declining then it should be viewed as a warning sign. It means that you have to start looking into your business to set it up right. Issues to look out for include stagnant sales, lowered profits, increase in expenditure, depreciation of assets, increase in the cost of goods sold, etc.

You must ensure that the profits your company is making are well within industry standards. If your company happens to be new, then look at the benchmark standards to determine how much you should ideally be earning. If it happens to be lower than standard then you should take matters in your hand and fix the issue.

If your company is showing a net loss, then here is an example that will help you understand how you can convert it to profit.

One reason your company can report a positive cash flow despite a net loss can be because of depreciation expense. Depreciation expenses tend to decrease a company's net income or rather, they end up increasing the net loss. It will not involve any cash payments in the current period. Say a business bought machinery in the previous year for a sum of $3,00,000 and it depreciates over the next ten years. Its depreciation expenses come up to $400,000. The current year's $400,000 entry will be done as a debit to depreciation expense and a credit to accumulated depreciation. If the company's income statement now shows a loss of $50,000 post the $400,000 "cash-free" depreciation then its cash will go up by $450,000.

One other explanation for it is accrual accounting. A business has to mention its expenditure as they are incurred, and it is done before a corporation pays the outstanding bills. Say a company that has an accounting year ending December 31, 2017, can have a significant expense pending at the end of 2012 but its invoice is not due until January 2018. The net income will be reduced, but the business's cash will not be reduced.

Here is another example. A business will receive a deposit from a client in December 2016, but it will only earn the revenue in 2017. If this is the case then the business's money will increase in 2016, but its revenue and net income will not increase until 2017.

Chapter Five: B/S - What can Change to Improve Cash?

The cash flow statement is directly related to the balance sheet. A variation in the numbers of the cash flow statement will be a direct result of changes occurring in the balance sheet throughout the year. These changes in the balance sheet are the reason behind the numbers in the cash flow statement.

Although the balance sheet, cash flow statement and income statement are intertwined, they are independent to some extent.

The balance sheet changes happen to be the base to prepare cash flow statements. The changes in the assets, liabilities and the owner's equity are the sum in the cash flow statement. They are used to find the amount of cash flowing into the business, the earnings that are held on to, the net income and the dividend that is earned.

The cash that comes in through the operating activities is usually in the form of net income and adjustments are made to it to find the exact cash that is flowing in through these activities. Assets and liabilities that are a part of this section are those that are used for profit making in a business set up.

Here is an example - the accounts receivable asset is debited when the product is sold on a credit basis. The inventory account is credited as and when the cogs or 'cost of goods sold' expense is recorded. The accounts-payable report is accredited when those expenses have been recorded that have not been paid for.

Here are some of the rules for cash flow adjustments to the net income.

- An asset growth during a specific period will result in a reduction of cash flow from profit
- An asset decrease during a specific period will increase the cash flow from profit
- A liability drop during a specific period will result in a decrease of cash flow from profit
- A liability increase during a specific period will increase cash flow from profit

Taking these rules into account, any sum, say $200,000, used as a depreciation expenditure for a year can be taken as a positive adjustment or an addition to the net income. Recording the depreciation expenditure can help reduce the value of fixed assets that are being depreciated.

To be a little more specific, the depreciation that is recorded will increase the balance of the accrued depreciation account that is subtracted from the cost of the fixed assets. Recording this depreciation will not include cash transactions. The cash outlay will occur only when the business purchased assets that are being depreciated.

Chapter Six: Cash Flow Statement - What can Change to Improve Cash?

Cash flow is the lifeline of a business and the most important aspect to look into. Even if a company is doing extremely well, it has its business in line, its sales are on the rise, and it is making amazing profits, there can still end up having trouble if they do not manage the cash flow. In fact, such companies that are doing extremely well are first in line to be hit by cash flow issues, as they will have their guard down.

Say for example a company whose debts are yet to be paid and money from sales begins to come in then it will lead to cash flow issues. It will mean that the company will not be able to pay off bills and take on issues related to invariable and variable costs such as paying wages, bills and can also end up putting a question mark on the company's creditworthiness.

As a business owner, you must take certain steps to improve the cash flow. Here are some of them explained.

Lease out

One good way is by leasing out the equipment, land and supplies, as they can be quite expensive if you try to buy them. Now, you may think that this will be a somewhat reverse move as you will have to pay a monthly rental fee towards it, but it will only help you maintain consistent cash flow. If, however, your company has enough at its disposal to be able to buy equipment instead of leasing then you can consider buying some of the equipment that is used on a daily basis and renting those that are used once in a while. Leasing helps in improving cash flow to a large extent and can also help you write off lease payments as an expense.

Loans

Take loans to buy the equipment if you do not wish to borrow them. This too can help you save money and improve your cash flow.

Discounts

As you know, everybody loves to receive discounts. If some of your customers pay much before their due date then by offering them discounts you will create a great opportunity for you and your client. At the same time, you have to charge extra to all those who fail to pay you on time. This will set them right and help you recover your costs faster. Make sure you make it clear to them that those paying before the due date will get a discount and those paying late will be fined. These discounts can vary weekly, bi-monthly, etc.

Credit checks

You have to perform credit checks on customers who do not wish to pay you in cash. Conducting these can help you check if the customer has poor credit and you can write them off or know that you might not be able to receive credit on time. Even if you wish to make the sale, late credits will end up affecting your business's cash flow. If you do choose a sale even after knowing the customer's inability to pay on time, then make sure you ask for a high rate of interest.

Cooperative

You must try and do all that you can to improve your cash flow. One way is by thinking about the masses. Find other companies that think like you and pool in money and form a cooperative. You can then haggle together and get suppliers to reduce costs. This will help you save money and increase your cash flow.

Increase inventory

Take a look at all the inventory that you have. Look at the bestselling and worst selling products that you have. If some products are slow movers, then get rid of them instead of holding them, as they will end up pulling your business down. You can put them up for sale and offer a good discount so that they can be disposed of. Even if you feel like the product has much potential you should dispose it off to make way for newer products. You must think about the company and make the decision.

Send invoices

If you send out the invoices quickly then you will see that receivables are coming in much quicker. You have to work on it immediately and send out the invoices as soon as the sales are made. You can consider reducing the standard time taken to dispatch the invoices and try to cut it by half. For example, you can reduce it from 2 months to one month. Similarly, speed up all other processes associated with receiving money so that you remain with a consistent cash flow.

Change payment mode

Pay electronically as it will allow you to wait until the time the bill is due. This will buy you time and help you improve your cash flow. You can also consider making use of a business card or business credit to get a grace period and improve your cash flow. You might also receive cash back but make sure you do not pile up on the debt. Ask your company's banker for details and get a card that will work to your advantage.

Accept card payments

If you allow your clients to make payments using cards then you be able to receive the payments the next day or on time. You can also encourage online payments, as those too will help you get the payments done faster and on time.

Pay less

If you can strike up a friendship with the suppliers and be in their good books then you increase your chances of receiving better offers from them. Pay off your suppliers in advance so that they can give you a discount.

High-interest account

Consider opening a high-interest account, as they will give you more liquidity and a chance to grow your cash position. As soon as spare money comes in you can add it to the account to make it work in your favor.

Increase prices

Do not be afraid to increase the prices fearing that sales will go down. It is fine to experiment now and then to increase the cash flow. If you do not take the chance then you will not know whether it will pay off or not. So, take a risk and do it so that you can be happy knowing what the result is.

Consult an accountant

If you are unable to work it out and cannot increase your cash flow, then consider speaking with an accountant to make it easier for you. They will provide you with cash flow projections and help you know when to expect profits and expenses. Knowing these in advance can help you avoid phases when cash flow becomes an issue.

Cash flow analysis

A cash flow analysis can help you find the best months when the cash flows are at their highest. For example, sweaters will sell the most during winters or in December. A cash flow analysis will help you analyze the highs and lows and help you time your loan borrowings.

Credit line

Get a line of credit so that you are prepared for short-term emergencies. It can help you prepare for short-term debts and manage your cash flow. You can draw from your line of credit whenever you like and manage to have a consistent cash flow. In fact, if you have one then you need not take out loans and worry about having to pay excessive interest rates. You can save the money in a high-interest saving account.

Continuity sales

One good way of increasing cash flow is by making offers that will last one to two years or more. For example, you can offer a subscription deal and get people to subscribe to it. This will help you receive the cash up front. Your customers will likely choose these deals, as they will be cost-effective choices for them.

Efficiency

Boost your staff's efficiency by training them and equipping them with tools that can help them work better. This can help you improve cash flowing into your business.

Remember that cash is king and you must do all that it takes to maintain a consistent cash flow. If you think that your business is bound to experience great profits in the coming months, but you do not have enough cash to pay for expenses during that time then you will not be able to realize those profits. It is therefore essential to adopt some of the tricks mentioned above so that your business can maintain a consistent and healthy cash flow.

Chapter Seven: Summary

It is not easy to run a business and takes passion and persistence. It is tough to take care of all the expenses and keep track of all the money that comes in and goes out. You have to ensure that you are on top knowing everything and are aware of the different strategies that can be employed to make the most of your cash flow.

Sound financial discipline is a prerequisite to maintaining a good business. You have to be aware of everything that goes on in the business to be able to maintain a consistent cash flow.

There is still a lot of debate over the actual importance of the three financial documents viz. income statement, balance sheet and cash flow statement. All three are essential no doubt, but it is widely agreed that the cash flow statement is the most important of the three.

The cash flow statement is a combination of two financial statements. It combines the operating activities with changes that occur in the balance sheet of a company. It keeps an eye on the money that flows into the company.

The most critical section of the cash flow statement is the "cash flow operations" as it shows how much money a company is making through its main business. The cash flow statement makes a note of the profits and the losses and also the working capital. It makes changes in the assets and liabilities such as the accounts receivable, accounts payable and other such categories to check whether your business is doing well.

For example, say that your business earns a revenue of $2,000 in a month, but all the products are sold on credit, which means that you have still not received the cash for them. Say the total cash outlays are $1750 for the current period. Here, your income statement will show a profit of $250 ($2000 as the total earnings minus $1750 as expenses).

Meanwhile, the cash flow from operations has dropped to $1750 as the business must pay $1750 in cash but has not collected an offsetting balance from clients. This will increase the accounts receivables balance by $2,000.

On the other hand, assume that your company attracts $3,000 in cash payments but pays up $4,000 as an expense, and $1,000 is paid in cash during the current period with the remainder paid through accounts payable. In such a case, the income statement will show a loss of $1,000 and still the company will create a $1,000 positive cash flow.

This is because you paid $2,000 in cash but paid $1,000 in expenses thereby leaving a $1,000 in cash left behind. All this happens in the cash flow statement that would show a $2,000 loss that is offset by a $3,000 increase in the accounts payable section.

As you have read in the book, it is vital for managers to manage their working capital accounts to increase the cash flow.

The balance sheet happens to be one from the four important documents that need to be prepared by a company, and they are as follows:

- Balance sheet
- Income statement
- Cash flow statement
- Statement of stockholder's equity

The balance sheet showcases a company's assets, liabilities and stockholder's equity in the current period. The rest of the financial statements showcase for an extended period such as a year, two years, three years, etc. The balance sheet is better known as the statement of financial position and showcases the following equation

Assets is equal to liabilities plus stockholders' equity

Financiers go through the balance sheet to check the amount of a company's capital that is nothing but the amount of assets subtracted from the current liabilities. They also go through the assets and liabilities of the company to compare the stockholder's equity.

If a balance sheet shows an item in an additional column from an earlier date then it is known as a comparative balance sheet.

Most companies issue a classified balance sheet that represents amounts in the following categories.

Assets

- Current assets
- Investments
- Property, plant, and equipment
- Intangible assets
- Other assets
- Total assets

Liabilities and stockholder's equity liability

- Current liabilities
- Noncurrent liabilities

- Total liabilities

Stockholder's equity

- Total liabilities and stock holder's equity

Here is a look at them in detail

Current assets

Current assets include cash and other assets that are said to turn into cash within a stipulated period say one year. Some common examples of current assets include cash and cash equivalents, short-term investments, inventory, etc.

Investments

Investments are noncurrent or better known as long-term assets. Long-term investments such as bond funds; real estate and cash reserved for plant and equipment are included.

Property, plant, and equipment

This category includes noncurrent assets including the likes of the cost of land, machinery, equipment, fixtures, machines, vehicles and other business operatives. Apart from land, everything will depreciate or go down in value over the course of time.

Intangible assets

Intangible assets are those that include the likes of trademarks, patents, goodwill, copyrights and other such non-physical assets that are acquired at a cost. The sum of their cost is arrived at after subtracting any amortization or writing off due to impairment. Trademarks and logos that are owned by the company are usually not reported as they are not purchased and are owned by the company.

Other assets

Here, costs that have been paid for but are expensed over a period of time that is over one year is recorded. Some of these include bonds that are issues and deferred income taxes.

Current liabilities

Current liabilities are pending debts of a business that is to be paid within a year of the date when the balance sheet is prepared. It will need a current asset or should be replaced with another current liability. These current liabilities include the likes of loan payable that will have to be paid within a year of preparing the balance sheet, accounts payable, tax payable and other such liabilities that are taken as expenses.

Noncurrent liabilities

These are long-term liabilities and will not be due for the next one year at least from the time the balance sheet is made. Some examples include the likes of equipment loans, bonds payable, deferred income tax, etc.

Stockholder's equity

This part of the balance sheet contains the following

- Paid in capital- the sum paid by investors to acquire original shares of the company
- Retained earnings-the earnings earned by the corporation since it started minus the sum that was distributed in the form of dividends
- Treasury stock- a deduction that shows the total sum to be paid to buyback the company's stock

Income statement

An income statement is better known as a statement of operations or a profit and loss statement and shows a company's revenue, expenses, losses and total income for a specific period of time say a year, two years, etc.

Format for income statement

There are two formats for income statement, and they are as follows

- Multiple step
- Single step

The difference between the two is that the number of deductions and totals that appear on the income statement before going to the net income.

Multiple step income statements are those where the following take place

- The first deduction will give a gross profit
- The second deduction will give an operating income
- The third deduction will provide a net income

Single step format is where the income statement will have just one deduction. Operating and non-operating incomes will be subtracted. There will be no subtotal for the gross profit or the operating income. The net income comes the as a single deduction.

Balance sheet and income statement correlation

Revenues are responsible for stockholder's equity to rise while the expenses cause stockholder's equity to go down. It is, therefore, a positive income that is shown on the income statement that causes stockholders' equity to rise. A negative net income will show a stockholder's equity to go down.

Income accounts are temporary and can be closed at the end of the accounting year. The correlation between the balance sheet and the income statement will help the business owners in knowing the net income that will appear in the income statement.

Conclusion

I thank you once again for choosing this book and hope you had a good time reading it. The primary aim of this book was to educate you on the basics of cash flow and show you how you can use it to enhance your financial position.

As you can see, there are quite a few things that you can do to present a positive picture. You can go through the book again to understand the concepts better.

I thank you again.